IT'S TIME TO LEARN ABOUT COELACANTH FISH

It's Time to Learn about Coelacanth Fish

Walter the Educator

Silent King Books
A WhichHead Entertainment Imprint

Copyright © 2025 by Walter the Educator

All rights reserved. No part of this book may be reproduced in any manner whatsoever without written per- mission except in the case of brief quotations embodied in critical articles and reviews.

First Printing, 2024

Disclaimer

This book is a literary work; the story is not about specific persons, locations, situations, and/or circumstances unless mentioned in a historical context. Any resemblance to real persons, locations, situations, and/or circumstances is coincidental. This book is for entertainment and informational purposes only. The author and publisher offer this information without warranties expressed or implied. No matter the grounds, neither the author nor the publisher will be accountable for any losses, injuries, or other damages caused by the reader's use of this book. The use of this book acknowledges an understanding and acceptance of this disclaimer.

It's Time to Learn about Coelacanth Fish is a collectible early learning book by Walter the Educator suitable for all ages belonging to Walter the Educator's Time to Eat Book Series. Collect more books at WaltertheEducator.com

USE THE EXTRA SPACE TO TAKE NOTES AND DOCUMENT YOUR MEMORIES

COELACANTH FISH

Way down deep where light is dim,

It's Time to Learn about
Coelacanth Fish

A strange old fish begins to swim.

With lumpy scales and fins so grand,

A fossil fish from ages long.

But then one day in ocean blue,

They found it swimming, yes, it's true!

It lived when dinosaurs would stomp,

Through steaming jungles, wet and swamp.

But still it swims in deep-sea caves,

A living fossil in the waves.

It's not like fish you often see,

Its fins are jointed, just like me!

They move like arms and legs would bend,

Which makes it really hard to trend!

Its color's dark, a bluish hue,

With white spots sprinkled here and through.

Its eyes glow green in ocean night,

It hunts for food without much light.

The Coelacanth is not so fast,

It's Time to Learn about
Coelacanth Fish

It drifts and glides, it doesn't dash.

It even does a flip or spin,

And sometimes floats with just a grin.

It hides all day in rocky cracks,

And hunts at night for little snacks.

Squid and fish it loves to munch,

With quiet gulps, it eats its lunch.

Its babies grow inside so slow,

Then out they come, all set to go!

No eggs laid out in sand or shell,

They're born alive and swim quite well.

So rare it is, we must take care,

And leave it be in deep-sea lair.

We study it, but from afar

This ancient fish, a shining star!

It's Time to Learn about
Coelacanth Fish

So now you know this fishy friend,

From ancient times that never end.

The Coelacanth is quite the tale

A mystery with a waving tail!

ABOUT THE CREATOR

Walter the Educator is one of the pseudonyms for Walter Anderson. Formally educated in Chemistry, Business, and Education, he is an educator, an author, a diverse entrepreneur, and he is the son of a disabled war veteran. "Walter the Educator" shares his time between educating and creating. He holds interests and owns several creative projects that entertain, enlighten, enhance, and educate, hoping to inspire and motivate you. Follow, find new works, and stay up to date with Walter the Educator™ at WaltertheEducator.com

www.ingramcontent.com/pod-product-compliance
Lightning Source LLC
LaVergne TN
LVHW051920060526
838201LV00060B/4094